BABIES AT THE ZOO

3

Chimpanzee Babies

Susan H. Gray

Published in the United States of America by
Cherry Lake Publishing
2395 South Huron Parkway, Suite 200, Ann Arbor, MI 48104
www.cherrylakepublishing.com

Content Advisor: Dominique A. Didier, Professor of Biology, Millersville University
Reading Advisor: Marla Conn, MS, Ed, Literacy specialist, Read-Ability, Inc.

Photo credits: ©KaWe-pictures/Shutterstock.com, front cover; ©Nick Biemans/Shutterstock.com, 1, 2; ©LiaoZhuangDjiu/Shutterstock.com, 4; ©Nataliia MelnychukShutterstock.com, 6; ©Carolyn Smith1/Shutterstock.com, 8; ©Mohammed younos/Shutterstock.com, 10; ©Charlotte Bleijenberg/Shutterstock.com, 12; ©zulfachri zulkifli/Shutterstock.com, 14; ©ben landy/Shutterstock.com, 16; ©Jeannette Katzir Photog/Shutterstock.com, 18; ©Phil O'nector/Shutterstock.com, 20

Library of Congress Cataloging-in-Publication Data

Names: Gray, Susan Heinrichs, author.
Title: Chimpanzee babies / written by Susan H. Gray.
Description: Ann Arbor, Michigan : Cherry Lake Publishing, 2020. | Series: Babies at the zoo | Includes index. | Audience: Grades K-1
Summary: "Read about the smart and social chimpanzee babies and how zookeepers take care of them. This level 3 guided reader book includes intriguing facts and adorable photos. Students will develop word recognition and reading skills while learning about how these baby animals learn and grow, what they eat, and how they socialize with each other. Book includes table of contents, glossary, index, author biographies, sidebars, and word list for home and school connection"—Provided by publisher.
Identifiers: LCCN 2019034086 (print) | LCCN 2019034087 (ebook) | ISBN 9781534158900 (hardcover) | ISBN 9781534161207 (paperback) | ISBN 9781534160057 (pdf) | ISBN 9781534162358 (ebook)
Subjects: LCSH: Chimpanzee—Infancy—Juvenile literature. | Apes—Infancy—Juvenile literature. | Zoo animals—Infancy—Juvenile literature.
Classification: LCC SF408.6.A64 G73 2020 (print) | LCC SF408.6.A64 (ebook) | DDC 599.88513/92—dc23
LC record available at https://lccn.loc.gov/2019034086
LC ebook record available at https://lccn.loc.gov/2019034087

Cherry Lake Publishing would like to acknowledge the work of the Partnership for 21st Century Learning, a Network of Battelle for Kids. Please visit http://www.battelleforkids.org/networks/p21 for more information.

Printed in the United States of America
Corporate Graphics

Table of Contents

About the Author

Susan H. Gray has a master's degree in zoology. She has written more than 150 reference books for children and especially loves writing about animals. Susan lives in Cabot, Arkansas, with her husband, Michael, and many pets.

Life in the Group

Chimpanzees are friendly animals. They live in groups. They eat and sleep together.

Chimpanzees live in Africa. Some live in zoos.

Do you like the same kinds of food that chimpanzees like?

Chimps spend most of their days eating and resting. They eat fruit, berries, and leaves from trees. Chimpanzees also eat **termites** and other bugs.

Usually, chimpanzee mothers have one baby at a time. A **newborn** is half the size of a human baby. It has thin, black fur.

The newborn is **helpless** and cannot walk. It **clings** to its mother's fur. The baby rests on her chest and drinks her milk.

Chimps at the Zoo

Sometimes chimps are born in zoos. These babies get lots of attention. **Zookeepers** check that they get enough milk and sunshine.

What can you see when you climb a tree?

Young chimps stay close to their mothers. But sometimes they **explore**. Zookeepers watch them closely. They might even watch them all night!

New Things

When a chimp is around 4 years old, things change. It stops sleeping with its mother. And it no longer drinks her milk.

Now it must find its own food. The chimp is known for being **clever**. It figures out how to peel bananas. It even learns how to crack nuts!

A female lives in a group her whole life. She has her first baby when she is about 13 years old.

A new, furry little chimpanzee!

Find Out More

BOOK

Llewellyn, Claire. *Chimpanzees.* New York, NY: Kingfisher, 2015.

WEBSITE

National Geographic Kids—Chimpanzee
https://kids.nationalgeographic.com/animals/chimpanzee/#ap-chimpanzee-map.jpg
This site includes photos, a map, and baby chimp facts.

Glossary

chimps (CHIMPZ) also known as chimpanzees
clever (KLEV-ur) able to understand and do things quickly
clings (KLINGZ) holds tightly
explore (ik-SPLOR) travel around in order to discover new things
helpless (HELP-lis) cannot take care of oneself
newborn (NOO-born) an animal that was born recently
termites (TUR-mites) small, soft-bodied insects that eat wood
zookeepers (ZOO-kee-purz) people who take care of zoo animals

Home and School Connection

Use this list of words from the book to help your child become a better reader. Word games and writing activities can help beginning readers reinforce literacy skills.

a
about
Africa
all
also
and
animals
are
around
at
attention
babies
baby
bananas
being
berries
black
born
bugs
but
can
cannot
change
check
chest
chimp
chimpanzee
chimpanzees
chimps
clever
climb
clings
close
closely
crack
days
do
drinks
eat
eating
enough
even
explore
female
figures
find
first
food
for
friendly
from
fruit
fur
furry
get
group
groups
half
has
have
helpless
her
how
human
in
is
it
its
kinds
known
learns
leaves
life
like
little
live
lives
longer
lots
might
milk
most
mother
mothers
must
new
newborn
night
no
now
nuts
of
old
on
one
other
out
own
peel
resting
rests
same
see
she
size
sleep
sleeping
some
sometimes
spend
stay
stops
sunshine
termites
that
the
their
them
these
they
thin
things
time
to
together
tree
trees
usually
walk
watch
what
when
whole
with
years
you
young
zoo
zookeepers
zoos

Fast Facts

Habitat: Forests and grasslands
Range: Africa
Height: 3 to 5.5 feet (91 to 168 centimeters)
Weight: 70 to 130 pounds (32 to 59 kilograms)
Life Span: 40 to 45 years in the wild, up to 60 years in zoos
Anatomy: The hair on the backs of older chimps turns gray.
Behavior: Chimpanzees use sticks as tools to collect food and check out possible dangers.

Index